Twenty-One After Days

Twenty-One After Days

Lisa Lubasch

Avec Books

Penngrove

I am grateful to the editors of the publications in which poems from this book first appeared, occasionally in earlier versions and with slightly different titles: "[literary strands – flit bemused – about the house]" in *American Letters & Commentary;* "[lampshades will admit of the spectacular]" in *Boston Review;* "[a theory is drawn]" in *The Brooklyn Rail;* "[this in branch will catch]," "[winter enters fretfully]," and "[Lightness is unfolding]" in *Coconut;* "[the rivers snatch up all our true developments]," "[With the lyrical observation, growing thinner]," "[separating, when we are staring]," "[wishing, almost grasping]," and "[startled – out of place]" in *Explosive Magazine;* "[certain modes of solitude – are experienced – as freedom]" in *The Hat;* "[out of inventiveness – looking]" in *Jubilat;* "[the morning is condensed – but it grows stale]" in *LIT;* "[the increment begins]" in *26 Magazine.* Thanks to Douglas Messerli for including "[a theory is drawn]" in *The Gertrude Stein Awards 2005-2006.* And thanks to Lena Goarnisson, Jacques André, and Olivier Brossard for publishing a French translation of "[lampshades will admit of the spectacular]" in *Arsenal,* with additional thanks to the translators, Ladislas Karsenty and Oriane Monthéard. – L.L.

ISBN: 1-880713-37-3
Library of Congress Control Number: 2005908764

Cover artwork by David Hockney
Window, Grand Hotel, Vittel, 1970
Crayon on paper, 17" x 14"
© David Hockney

Avec Books
P.O. Box 1059
Penngrove, CA 94951

Printed in the United States of America on acid-free paper

Contents

One – 9

Two – 23

Three – 33

Four – 47

Five – 63

ONE

lampshades will admit of the spectacular – are they hosts to other things? – greedy narratives – where the poem boils over – rings on the bed, so the surrounding bets are off – influence may also be a wanderer of sorts – clandestine raveler – these mincing ways that words go in – where sea habitations co-exist – variations of the same dress gathered – we grow subtle – in the narrations of our fingers – it all goes well – enough – by being rubbed into consensus – as omissions would slide – across a pillow – or a window – where you are sitting – at the table, she was speaking about her "arrival" as a sculptor – in two countries – literally two on either side – a lot of people spoken there in British English – which has replaced Afrikaans – and the roosters always crowing starting at five – when somnolence cracks – irritating the gust – it is difficult to comprehend – the arrogance in her hair – or the signal places – that imagination alters – though its glance is glass – right where looking accomplishes – automatic sweep – a given hillside twitching – out of visibility – nuances coincide, but at any moment – you may be shouldered out – never forget this – said the bragging participant – just before asking – what rhymes with death? – sayeth – what rhymes with orange? – in the airport lounge – blond hair pinned back – a pair of hurried feet – any perception would catch – and be an aphrodisiac – as intelligence also admits – of being captured – or milling about – all in a single act – but the inference is unnerved – parts company – exactly on her birthday – where I sit to where – the white roots are – qualitatively whiter – infinite in their capture – and the distance is traveled – as force of distance underwrites the letter – scrawled across the doorway to the Gecko coffee shop – cross the *t* and dash the *i* – of candles lit and needles catching . . .

o o o o

this in branch will catch – far laughing – the leaf is nought – in the purposeful day – where painting grows by drizzle –

in the book, his name in the index spelled with missing *c*'s – coaxed out of late – admiration through – as the exposure is tripping under us – saturated with our attentions – pursued by sympathy – deliberately, waving itself across – twin predictions of the same coast –

but the bird on her shoulder was chirping at a deafening pitch – its outer aspect thinning – to disquieting shades of zero – later – there was no going over it – one long hollow, and methodically – transcribed – the description was selfish – in the mouth of the betrothed

o o o o

the rivers snatch up all our true developments – making them square, as methodically day would – gather up its lineaments – one promontory competes (couples) with the inventory – for confidence – will we meet? to the right of it? – that depends – as migratory gulls would spark – retrieve their careful rims – making them truthful – only outwardly, however – the thing inside will loose its breath – growing very casual over time – so much so that the narration takes on a pallor – almost owning it – the attrition shows a tender reversal – gloomy arrows, ripped of their concerns – raising care to the level of error –

but patience may bloom backward into knowledge – covered in nettles – and bannering spirals – and the sleepy eye is shaded – for a time – from spotting – who darkening travels towards the exemplary ear – though his skirts and hills are adjusted – to fit the flattening scene – each person – could and would be culpable – is that disingenuous? – on a desk, or in a congregation, three – fluencies of course, culling – their articulable beads – dew on rocks, on the gardenias you bought – and took pictures of – sifting, asserting their necks – aphoristically – the color is admitted – as a match to sleep, but wait – it should complete the scene more fully – if you urge it towards the red – for many years, I kept these looks together – blending them with shades of indiscretion

o o o o

trails – lingering – on the brink of a conjecture – what is imminent is the chasing – to conceptualize the cold – which is stalled in place – and cannot be amended – like a given phenomenon will uproot – become upheaval over time – all content blown out – or converted into sanitized enjoyment – sanitized as lack or inexpression – but not wanting to dip into that yet – as each day, any moment of perversion – or adhesion – would be cultivated and buried – and only then – if you are counting – if you are tricked into the sum – by one bloodhound – and three anemic relatives – three as the nearest number – that fancy's wraith has courted – the pining for delay – another source of shiver – and relief – and yet that's clearly not the only story – if you begin with truth – there's almost nothing left – by lunch

o o o o

strife will produce accomplishments – inadvertently – like sleep or mildness – will reduce the course of feeling – its amount, merely an incidental factor – its rose is cold and nearly ocular – vehicular – where splitting occurs – becoming metaphor – in lists – conversation – cuts off – the spectacle admitted through rocks . . . –

it is all a manner of sparking – accruing – a subtraction – where irritants spell out – mushy shapes, fruits on the bough – certain precepts, too, their iridescent features – almost eroding, as displeasure – its inward strings grown out – accidentally pressed – into the impersonation of facts – one place, in particular, fetching – the sewing on her shirt – and pairs of shoes – just competent enough – to make a convincing argument – about consistency –

is it because the glen isn't wide enough – to accommodate *The Complete Poems*? – that coughs will moisten or fume – of pressed and lemony powder – melancholy may be guarded – inwardness as shift – so states renew and become dazzling

o o o o

its lights are brimming – the cursor is dragged – speech is taking – irritating turns, it goes swimming at each chance – a necessary tongue – not genuinely confessed – its beginning – a triangle – a side the length of any fraction – she complicates the logic – immediately perceived in the immense – flexibility of objects – nonetheless – its nerves are crocheted together – interrupted by a portion without clouds

o o o o

winter enters fretfully – is diverted – murmuring – almost without frond – climbing up,
where the finish is – as often values – acquire translucency – in drifts of sills and locks – become
as interference – frost contracts – and readies for transition – leveling out all prospects – as the
cycles turned – they were compared – to apprehend the difference – as I recall – and the whitening
of the book – in which example – pleased itself with placing – frames of laughing in a tighter stall
– though each element would be worried out – and further still – arranged in sleep – the cat
embarrassed – or growing violent, even, in a certain climate – where it sleets more often –

but once you get hooked, you may never want to grieve – the shrieking culmination of stars –
and weedy bird – always the somnambulist – a virulent track – of verdurous sun – over counter
– smugly approaching in unfinished quality – trespassing – as we shall show – as it shall be
detected – now inside, students are examining – chains of admonishment – to rule out the larger
context – centered in an immediate past – as persistence drips out – to inundated cores – drearily,
on either side – producing neither glorification nor regret – but something narrower in conception
– the presupposition lost – as ambition is swept up, orienting itself around a place – a wish, a
force of heft – in acknowledgment

o o o o

the morning is condensed – but it grows stale – its rigor becomes a subject – tearing – meaning flows out – birds fly up and grow to skip within – a mountain – one part of it – the breezy section, augmented – a break in confidence occurs – delayed, diverted, and collapsed – contrasted with other figures – as divisions arrange themselves – on a vertical hill – losing its green color, right at the top – of the scenario – another is ripping – or hemmed within – a narrowly occurring idea – the element out the window – flying into parts – concessions are made – to land or tree – the wind goes by – we think about ending – possibly – monumental and exposed – the maggoty walk up – to an opening in the day – rains fall in – tireless motions of uncertainty . . . – all dreams – dark – heavy – broken conversations – haphazardly seeing – the eye is spinning – conflict occurs – detracts – from the vigor – the yes is felt as truth – we melt into guessing – concentration cowers – simplicity – a sideways effect – a moment of – vivid scars and inert descriptions – resembling in shape – in thought submerged – a pure reiteration – myriads of notes – lucidly – appearing – the interior – escaping – unhooked as weight

∘ ∘ ∘ ∘

With the lyrical observation, growing thinner, or growing nostalgic, slippery of judgment, and

distancing ourselves, in conversation with a leaf, in steps, our obvious desire, to make a theater

of our concerns, to make the redress, poignant, in understanding of it, its life pulled back,

redemptive, the fact of it, orange, a sinuousness, reaching out beyond privacy, of recollection,

turning towards rhapsody, distilled, laid inside a box, marked, on the inside, mistaking not one's

movement as achievement, but taking it as, the brightening of one's conceptions, curling in wind,

hovering, entries, as decisions will permit, the primordial current, to reach an ordinary aim, and

so grow involved, with our attempts at understanding, whose monotony is scarring, graying itself

up, with an inward, an outward, heaviness, of identity, of stillness,

Then a blanketing would occur, upon the earth, as splendor, translucency, yards of us running,

steadily, wedded, to an inner logic, the field misted, filled, with condemnation, currents, yielding,

to an account, by necessity, an outlook, an unavoidable inference, made systematically, the affair,

in error, whose pace would seize, whose glance would be detected, distending, matted, into the

sphere of cautions, roots, flowers flapping back and forth, flown in the sky, and cruelty, its

frequency, stuttered, along a furrowed ridge, of growth and matter, slippery, we would set off,

in a direction, embarking, upon a path, a rock, where an icicle has molded, we would grow, in

disappointment, that love, was never, offered, only spoken, in accounts,

The body, slippery, is a script, walking, penitently, all abandonment, is in turn, metrical, a

complaint, launched, branched out of it, traced a new direction, a tree has risen, loneliness, that love

was never, across a rock, sunlight, spoken in accounts, waiting, penitently, for the concise,

and articulable current, pressing to complete, the opinion, about how, about what, we would then

be finished, in our own, ardent register, saliency, on lips, at one remove, in the distance,

This in our opinion, this abandonment, has its own ardent register, the lake would inwardly contract, pressed, tender, conversant with the rain, falling, at indeterminable speeds, bleeding, occurring, imagined, as an aftereffect

o o o o

out of inventiveness – looking – the clock has strayed – abandonment – bleached as day, its underside – where the fact is suffocated – submerged – defended from moral obligation – all accessories fading – in rushed revisions – light is tracing – scripting – lies are fancied – beneath awnings – and become relentless – indefatigable chords – trimmed from mouths – or lines of entries – the vision is idling – on the river – over woods, abundantly – a slippery concern – is riled – to contain abandonment – shifting – out of consonance – and anemic – in its fathering – thrown out with the trees – and the gusts – a redundant longing – in decline – all projects growing dim – hard to return to – but trying – deceptive in their celibacy – deliberate, narrowed – out of all approval – in memory – demanding – whimpering – to unearth the splendor – of the path – conceptual or curdled – I – right there in the month – leaves are showing – their triumphant signals – luminous scatter – unaware – of other diverse events – their meager capacity – for astonishment – barren ideas – loosing themselves from – legitimate reception – and so content to stutter vaguely – inside a meaningless hour – of lapsing – and converging – the day beside us – shading – in the course of its contention – which has withered – which has turned

o o o o

the sun is setting, in astonishment, plotting out our sums, though the sight is difficult to render, energized or lacking, flights of aggression, the flights are, beckoning to contain, differing, counting out our sums, all the time subtracting, linking, in an hour, in a letter, blunder and attack, unnavigable, what is done, vast concentration of dark purpose, condemned, the look is shadowed, faded, presence, is thirsting, has a value, case and number, the physiognomy noted, to the letter, what is done, a value or a case, a number, tears, blunder and attack, the plane of our approach, the vine, jostled unawares, from sleeping, perhaps, obscenely turning, slanting towards a worry, the entry is concealed, is suppressed

Two

the increment begins – but inward time – is surreptitious – an amalgam – carried – in doubt
– lodged – deepening – where the premise sticks – a single detail has departed – is draping – is
fixed as a diagonal – militant – through the window – under the vine – listening is demanded –
the sun is – growing inwardly – tense – to speak – of beginning – to fit the concept – momentarily
– its understanding – intends a pattern – suspicion builds – in anticipation – of enjoyment, of
other states – is immediately bound – to sinister fruits –

its spans – measured – distances – drawn upon the snow – with a marble hand – inside a
clamoring cloud – withered branch – grown towards other cadences – shades of gathering –
mapped – to insinuate the sleeper – one garden – the prospect of another – seeming to weep
– to reveal – a quality – a color – a meeting place –

flimsy entries – winter is – incinerated – an artificial boundary – sympathy – now grows faint –
light settles – within the space of an afternoon – played apart – through the door – sudden
indecisiveness – delinquency – made to sink – to grow regressive – to draw – or make conclusive
– other faculties – inside the self – once merely – quixotic moments – one grew passionate about
– innocently later – standing – at the water – its reflection – suspicion –

the reenactment – barred – lifting in the water – so the reflection is dissolved – no, flourishing –
as if in some agreement – evolving – slowly becoming a worry or a friend – a monument or a
flickering form – finicky as stars – to make the concept swoop – a question – it lapses – the
grammar of the action – could be stalled – insularity – the heart – the aridness – gives example –

as weariness – admits of growing – it tows – the rooms of the house – your confidence is divided – between charity and majesty – between several chapters – in all earnestness – here and now – as one is telling of – the loosening of the barrier – discretion – presses gently – up to the mind – up to the border of freedom – or to its suggestion – this blinking passes for life – and one is fearful – the quietness is furnished

○ ○ ○ ○

Where weariness is, sunlight resuscitates, growing into rims of inattention. Clouds are booths, redundancies, shapes. Marks are drawn, so centers can be formed. Rows of shops, where pleats are flown. It is not as in the center, though bleeding of doorways occurs, ruffling the space on the outer side. Or sliding, trickling, a pirouetted number. Shoots of flowers off a band of rocks, a recitation of the way things converge. In a hand. In back of the house. That is where the rivers are, tides drawing in and rowing out. Streams draw and combine. Slide and scale, though lucid bits are culled and brought to rest. A lamp is reading, producing a devastating effect. Pricked and stilled.

o o o o

certain modes of solitude – are experienced – as freedom – but cannot be sustained in that capacity – so are introduced – to new impediments – as someone will be – strict – or alternatively caring – looking out a pane – ignoring – simultaneously – other aspects of a situation – spread out across the morning –

a fable flies across – misted – sliding itself out of doors – thinking aloud – in the trees – there, you see – one can take on airs – if only for a moment – and for the purpose of achieving – states of relaxation –

as the telling is rolled – off the course – which contains the pronoun – and the asterisk – for reasons guessed but seldom noted – the path of safety lies with such distraction – half-practicing itself – all the rules of thumb – in mimic of yellow – found in many flowers – recorded in privacy – marked for resemblance – to categories of thought –

everything brought to the table – composed – moribund – yet still concerned with pleasure – (in ways children are) – beads of laughter – taking form – a simple demonstration – the acknowledged lark – cannot be trimmed to fit – it's drawing nigh and struggling to become

o o o o

separating,

when we are staring,

at figures,

erupting over the mountain,

the eye not stopping,

at water,

or at ledges,

until light drizzles in,

to mark and fix,

the horizon,

all concentration being,

this internal movement,

towards beauty,

if beauty resides,

in the form's suggestion,

a ray dips under day,

sleeves of it attain,

or yield to,

motion

                             o o o o

wishing, almost grasping,

at the point of thinning into an illusion,

loosening worry, from the water,

rolling over hills, amplifying,

and on the face of it, welling, opening in the sun,

the day, conjuring a fall,

one is tending, and intuiting the feeling,

or tinkering with, relationships between objects,

their lengths, conducted across a plane,

as all ideas are restless, to escape the obvious,

the innermost will, translates, possibly, or is coerced,

producing the sensation of fleeing,

into a desolate eye

o o o o

the sound is drifting, in the weather,

as day settles, her evolution comprehended freely,

in darkness, meeting involves, waiting, enduring what happens,

estranged from truce or letter,

in the sound, a facet of the rain is captured,

then dried up into a plainness,

unraveled, observation, like a tendril grazed diagonally,

lifting, where the gust is,

dispossessed of its own magnitude

THREE

Discursiveness enters,
is pulled
inside a net,

though my part in it has bounced,
become ignited
in the past.

Light is merging,
tending towards completion,
lucidly creating a figure unforeseen.

A group of followers
gathers on the lawn,
tripping and gathering

in the face of some potential freedom –
one must learn to
appear to bear the flurry. . . .

An evenness
conceals itself from every living thing,
nonetheless trying

to escape, as sunlight

gives a total sensation

of being-in-and-with, there-and-for,

and will mount

oh singly as tulips

that have freed themselves from erring. . . .

o o o o

Lately as the imperative mounts
towards the sun
(morning unchaining itself

from constancy),
it murkily invokes
its own despair:

Could momentum be lost
like a target
shaken from the wall?

Her eyes water,
gathering attributes
to create a true account,

whose language is
nonetheless
snatched, inherited.

The telling
is accruing
strands,

all products of compulsion,
its rivers and fluencies
going

against the wave of
evidence,
vaporous, susceptible . . .

Like ideas
and elements would vie,
coax themselves towards readiness,

the pose of expectancy –
the mother in waiting,
an alibi

grown complex.
As the desire
to shape her own anxiety

into recognizable form
causes her to grow patient,
intent.

o o o o

Inner resting

Can produce

A translation

Becoming very quickly

More quickly than

Barns peaking in error

Leaving all windows to the door

Though it's uncertain

That force

Is amplified as envy, or as

Vertical growth

They carve out

Some paths more than others

While also shaking their heads, *no* and *no*

Almost always, within patience

o o o o

Hovering there, on the sill,
as everything
moves towards revision . . .

On a cold day,
the mind blurs its points,
almost consuming them.

Still, any confession
grows into
corners. . . .

Loss of concentration
is a sign of loss
of cheer,

the prism through which
one studies
all requirements.

The room is unmoving,
but its punctuation
is stirred.

As names are cries and formulations,
we rehearse
catching.

This numberlessness
is bent on leaving,
sweeping, swimming

towards a divide.
We are submitting
all consolation and time, yielding,

aridness of the day
recurrent,
erased,

whispers opening
their plots
simultaneously.

o o o o

Eyes will not confess,
create an entrance.

If the sky is gray and welling,
bare and brimming,
eyes grow dim –

But the menace of their looking
goes unchanged –
it spins, gathering primacy.

∘ ∘ ∘ ∘

the moment – evolving – out of shape –

her look is – error – or concern –

speech – feverish or hassled –

in a rush – to let the entrance grow –

apprehensive – untoward –

continuance has turned – hollow –

as an echo –

the noise would not abate –

shaded – a tree inside the mist –

dampened – with introspection –

the surface of her interest – then escaping –

unlaced –

from inside – as the mind is –

pulled – cordoning off a place –

winter descends into –

sensing the annulment – of a long-forgotten chore –

a leaf – grows vacantly out – white – unremitting

о о о о

it stands in place – affirming its location in the field –

she – would ascribe traits to it – such as – fixity –

one way of saying –

that the first person – resists its own disruption –

a garden grows dysphoric –

just in time – for the snow –

which has settled unmistakably – upon the roofs –

self – reformulated as scribble –

its untoward aspect – diminishing –

startled – a murmur

∘ ∘ ∘ ∘

the voice

rehearsing at its boundaries

in through the door   and stops   a wave   clandestine   forward through the door

and stops

it curls   cuts into the rain   running at its vision   awkwardly   poised against the wind

or balked at   pressed against its circle

it tries to raise its pitch   to pitch the earth and circle   through the door   drenched

in its interior demand

caught   along the corridor   in its demand   a repetition   the uncomposable gesture

of its body   gone to mourning   gone to hills   abhorring   the absence of tenses

longing for   no letter

it cannot hear   its own   delicate pronouncement   abhorring   no letter   in its grieving

holds   a finger   it compresses   its attempts

it curls   cuts into the line

it cannot hear

a gesture   vain abundance

of its heart

FOUR

Lightness is unfolding,
a current
pressed

inside a breathing space
which is another's
chamber.

The space could be protective,
latticed,
perceived in steps,

and never-ending.
Or with an end
that nonetheless will spill

in the direction
of a cloud
and a river.

The river has emerged
in conditions of sadness,
in imitation of

abstract flowers,

which have themselves

grown wilted

in proportion

and resistance.

As a face is blown across

a vacancy

in the breath between reactions,

one breath at a time

scalding, effacing

her mission,

loath to call sincerity

into the pattern.

Into the next one.

As once a feeling was permissible,

though impossible.

Coughed up

into the mordant haze,

the baffling work of terms
flute-like in their influence,
all infinitives

recorded through the light of
one quickening eye
and lift of looking.

The look tends to lower
now towards the left,
now towards the middle,

then despairing
of aspiration,
of trying.

Trying will loom
over the store
of ends,

and sharpness will mar
fingers
in the service of entry,

each suffering acute,
even, perhaps, rigged
to fix the plan

or transcend it.
The subject is then stirred
towards a conclusion.

o o o o

a theory is drawn – susceptible – to turning – is unreliable –

one function of it – moves swiftly – unspeakably – like the urge to be born –

into the twin traits – of innocence and defiance –

sweeping them across – the rocks –

the green of standing – at a noticeable distance –

where one, in another –

is often an equation – one measure – of the standard –

figures converge – on a scene, disrupted –

her stare – across a pane –

advancing – against fragility

o o o o

Searching is distilled,

standing up – it tears –

admits its own precariousness –

Where each of the drives is

impurely – waiting on the platform –

leagues blowing into the vertical

Breeze – scrawled out –

wasted, cut –

an underlying premise.

o o o o

attempts – at an internal logic – keeping one within – the blinds down, so light passes through in slits, only – where number is inclined in a direction – then as noise is – slinking to caresses – but there are other forces – such as – the bald part of a flower – clinging – connected – to a stare – blurring – haplessly – fading its attention out –

nature is diverted – but only briefly – soon the weedy insincerity of things – attracts us – its sadness traced – across an incongruous scene – in which reasoning trails, is inverted – not to fit – it is like a symptom – or an effort at its remedy – through staying indoors – the course or lease of the action – contained within the present, the minute – observation occurs –

how unusual – that the bird would flit – and be the destination – of its own idea – as sleep is gathered in hand – or barred from the experience – and as experience engenders there – speculations – of remorse and value – concurrently – all days gather in on themselves – or are they – a limiting – of the attempt – at just the remedy?

o o o o

shapes of flowers contract – their initial obviousness – stilled – a limit to one's own distress – or like dulled experience – one flower softens and then starts to sink – into a river and its leaves –

premises scattered – fitfully, the mind hastens – painfully compelled – along an observation – its various points – mark out time – bent – split – staged – they will not come to rest –

not in water – where the birds are meddling – sunlight filtering – the sleuthing in the perception – in its gathering of aims – the exchange is – milked throughout the day – a mediocre ghost – or belief in one – as when nostalgically this word passes – estranged

o o o o

the word is unavoidable – it inflates a plot –

pressing aims – that come to form a verdict –

in silence – would settle –

into the falling of – rain swept through –

rebounding along paths –

apprehended – like a look –

that crowds out – sincerity – care – bleeding into error –

the imprecise action – alone –

wedded – to a possibility –

of deafness

∘ ∘ ∘ ∘

Tuning out other formal features
of enticement or inventiveness,
a phrase for listening underscores the force of

disappointment.
This disappointment is one feature
whose tides are introspective,

detached from the face
whose passion
for the plan is rife with difficulty,

whose accounts have a truthfulness,
despite the inimical looks,
allegiances, aims.

The whole face lowers its attention
onto the darting sky,
disconnected or attracted.

The trail is loosened,
vexed.
The mission has demanded

that we empty out our bodies,
then be rid of them,
like certain states

that are initial –
a meaning disentangles
from its own philosophy,

frost
on the window
confusing its claims.

As the day grows, I could
instill myself
if the feeling lifts.

○ ○ ○ ○

as identity fastens – loosely –

onto those we love and whom we echo – in absence –

loneliness settles –

revealing in the trees, where light has splintered –

enclosure, sun, or vein –

severance of each thing –

or "A LIFE, and nothing else" –

quiet on to the shore – driving her eye up to the inner condensation of clouds – a failed
recourse to gesture –

a tree closed off in evanescent longing – in each thing ceasing to occur –
an hourglass, or vestry

o o o o

Now that the figure is seen,
it is recorded as a worry, the dress of it
crumpled, dismissed, like shades of presence –
all suddenness drawn out

where looking
designates a nuance,
an infidelity. . . .

Then the river recalls itself
erasing the scheme.

FIVE

where this truth occurs, it is shifting,

turning into,

sheets of rain,

the figure of her certainty,

digested,

summoned out of presence,

just as she would,

rearrange her diary,

visually reorganizing its claims,

to make,

a less realistic account,

whose terror is,

more evident

o o o o

a promise grows – impure –

in the transfer –

to another –

it is – in its abjection –

reading its own hieroglyph – out of mourning – out of air –

understanding – only – identity –

it speaks – to an arrow – saying – "yes yes" –

anything to hear its voice –

repeatable – as a vacant room

o o o o

to name, not name, insist upon a name, to know or not be named, in the day, which has revived itself, imprinted itself upon an agreeable world, reaped the benefits, of saying, of lying, of . . . seeing what, in spite of asking and reversing . . . there you are, how came you here, how in the ever did you come, what to say, what lie . . . where the sunlight streaks into visibility, here on an outcast day, rustling, faltering, merging, free, lengthened inside an opening

○ ○ ○ ○

truth is staggered in a chance
as a name is stammered in difficulty
entered

where the meaning
of one person
is caught

the day is leashed
to words
and endings

the case of the
human
waking to a disinterested art

o o o o

literary strands – flit bemused – about the house –

rows of entries – faltering –

as love – in its education – and attrition –

it is also a matter – of the nature of one's own anxiety –

as one is – made to nurse a life of superstitions –

a life inherent – in objects themselves –

pale, irregular as shadow – as mystification in fact – or in idea – denatured –

giving the appearance of – what – we cannot say –

we cannot suffer –

we are veering – towards the same reconciliation –

our voyage – in advances – around the hill –

we have come to see – and not see – call and not call –

for sometimes a perception – travels through us –

we're unloosened – in its equivocal brightness –

our knowing is then changed –

gone from the afternoon's vista

o o o o

startled – out of place –

all accounts are – off course –

the letter is foolish – when it describes – her hope to contain – distance –

within the contours of a day – which has reached another point – an interruption –

her crime requires nothing – for comprehension –

some remorse discerning itself within the blank – a registration of motives –

for teasing – the one at the barn – the one at the landing – actually laughing –

or diminution is – a possibility –

emptiness – eyes as filters –

a gesture colored in or cast – (in the mirror) –

like a prospect or a garden – that's devised its inner lapse

o o o o

you move your attention,

never certain,

if it's care or blame,

that enters into the room,

that equates weight,

with meaning,

some unknown variable,

of the climate,

disinclined to tread,

the water's,

temperamental,

boundary,

vague conclusion of a clock,

or of a hawk,

the sky,

wagering nothing,

inexplicit,

in its reference,

leniency of,

her hand,

a thing less beautiful,

she writes,

intimate with,

disparity,

the veridical position,

erased,

outside the window,

in her blind spot,

the motive,

refusing to, clamoring to

o o o o

The visible re-enters. We crane our necks, light is moving,
the grimness of it runs –
where the motion occurs, you are trying to understand
semblance, more than shadow

on asphalt. Later, pouring one's frame of mind into a room –
the day is producing a course
and field of knowledge, rain, and worry –
an arrow, pointing at direct inversions of itself –

So the path of privacy burns out,
is retraced.

o o o o

It is loose, light settles in, and now it's yearning, it settles, the yarn would stall. Loosing itself from corridors, it is sewn into place, then ever around. What is notched is the acknowledgment. It is thin and working, as the lie scatters out. As numbers will.

The silence is skipping, skipping out across the banner of the field. It is in unison with number. It is skipped. Skipped and draping like the number on the field. Flowers are numbers, truly inescapable, if on a bridge and hurrying. As leaves exceed their landing points and then become collapsed. Ceasing, then, and winking. Where is the excitement? All enveloping. Albeit in a field, with the dreariness of rain. A call flutters by, like waking.

NOTE

p. 60: The quoted text is a fragment from *Pure Immanence: Essays on A Life* by Gilles Deleuze, translated by Anne Boyman (Zone Books, 2001). In its entirety, the sentence reads, "We will say of pure immanence that it is A LIFE, and nothing else."

About the Author

LISA LUBASCH'S previous collections of poetry are *To Tell the Lamp* (Avec Books, 2004), *Vicinities* (Avec, 2001), and *How Many More of Them Are You?* (Avec, 1999), which received the Norma Farber First Book Award from the Poetry Society of America. She is the translator of Paul Éluard's *A Moral Lesson* (Green Integer Books) and with Olivier Brossard, works by Fabienne Courtade and Jean-Michel Espitallier, among others. Selections from *How Many More of Them Are You?* were translated into French in 2002 and appear as a chapbook in Un bureau sur l'Atlantique's Format Américain series. She lives in New York City.